P9-DFJ-464

Mrs. Mathis

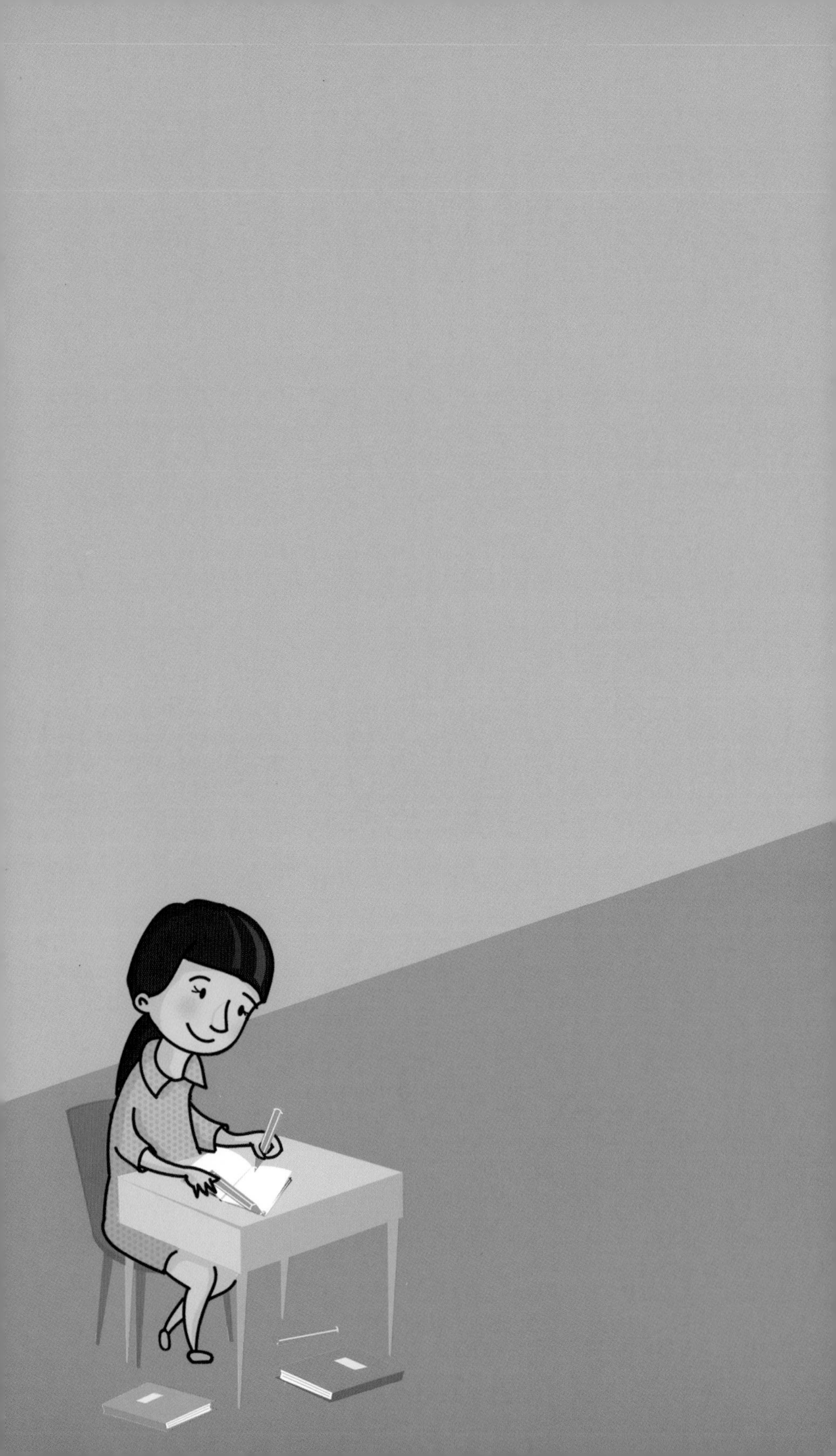

FIRST GRAPHICS

# MANNERS MATTER IN THE CLASSROOM

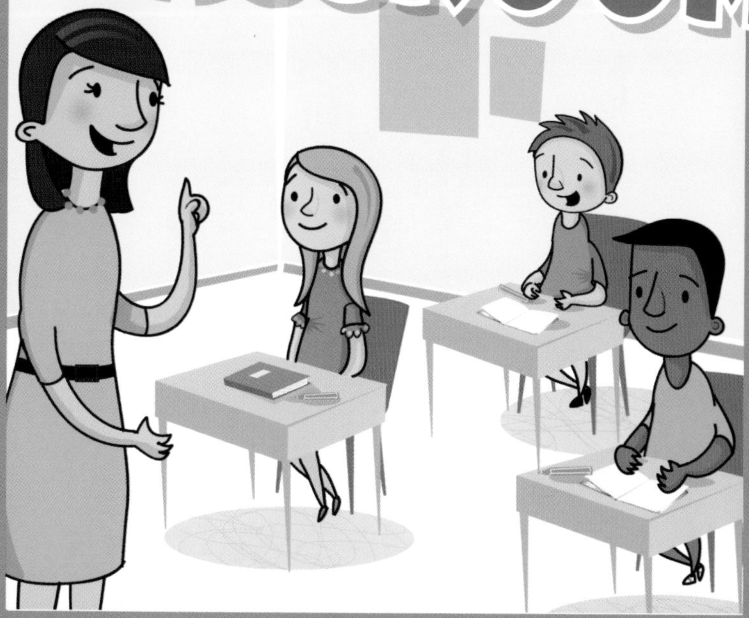

BY LORI MORTENSEN

ILLUSTRATED BY
Lisa Hunt

CAPSTONE PRESS
a capstone imprint

First Graphics are published by Capstone Press,
1710 Roe Crest Drive, North Mankato, Minnesota 56003.
www.capstonepub.com

Copyright © 2011 by Capstone Press, a Capstone imprint. All rights reserved.
No part of this publication may be reproduced in whole or in part, or
stored in a retrieval system, or transmitted in any form or by any means,
electronic, mechanical, photocopying, recording, or otherwise, without
written permission of the publisher.
For information regarding permission, write to Capstone Press,
1710 Roe Crest Drive, North Mankato, Minnesota 56003.

Library of Congress Cataloging-in-Publication Data
Mortensen, Lori, 1955–
  Manners matter in the classroom / by Lori Mortensen ; Illustrated by Lisa Hunt.
    p. cm. — (First graphics)
  Includes bibliographical references and index.
  ISBN 978-1-4296-5333-6 (library binding)
  ISBN 978-1-4296-6223-9 (paperback)
  1. Etiquette for children and teenagers—Juvenile literature. 2. Elementary schools. 3.
Graphic novels. I. Hunt, Lisa (Lisa Jane), 1973– , ill. II. Title. III. Series.

BJ1857.C5M67 2011
395.5—dc22

                                    2010026607

Editor: **Shelly Lyons**
Designer: **Juliette Peters**
Art Director: **Nathan Gassman**
Production Specialist: **Eric Manske**

Printed in China.
092011      006354R

# TABLE OF CONTENTS

# Mind Your Manners

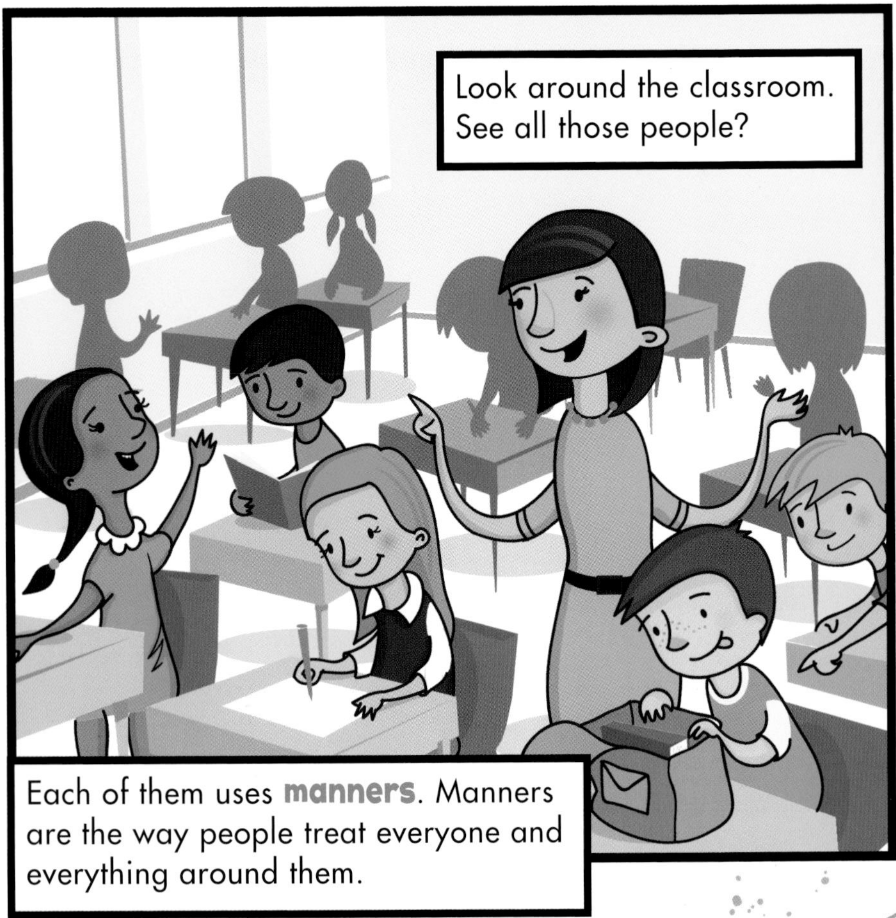

Look around the classroom. See all those people?
Each of them uses **manners**. Manners are the way people treat everyone and everything around them.


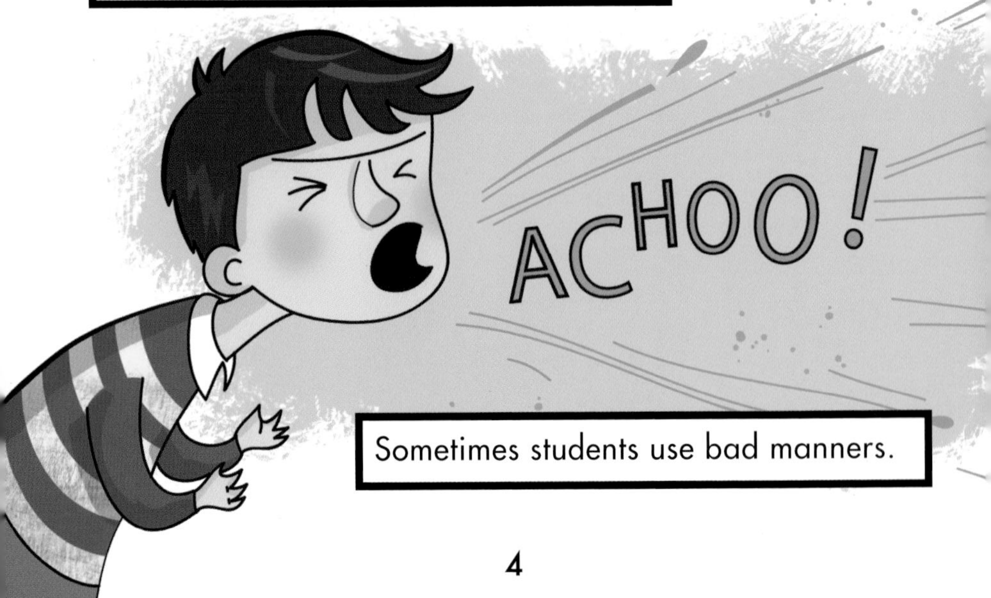

ACHOO!
Sometimes students use bad manners.

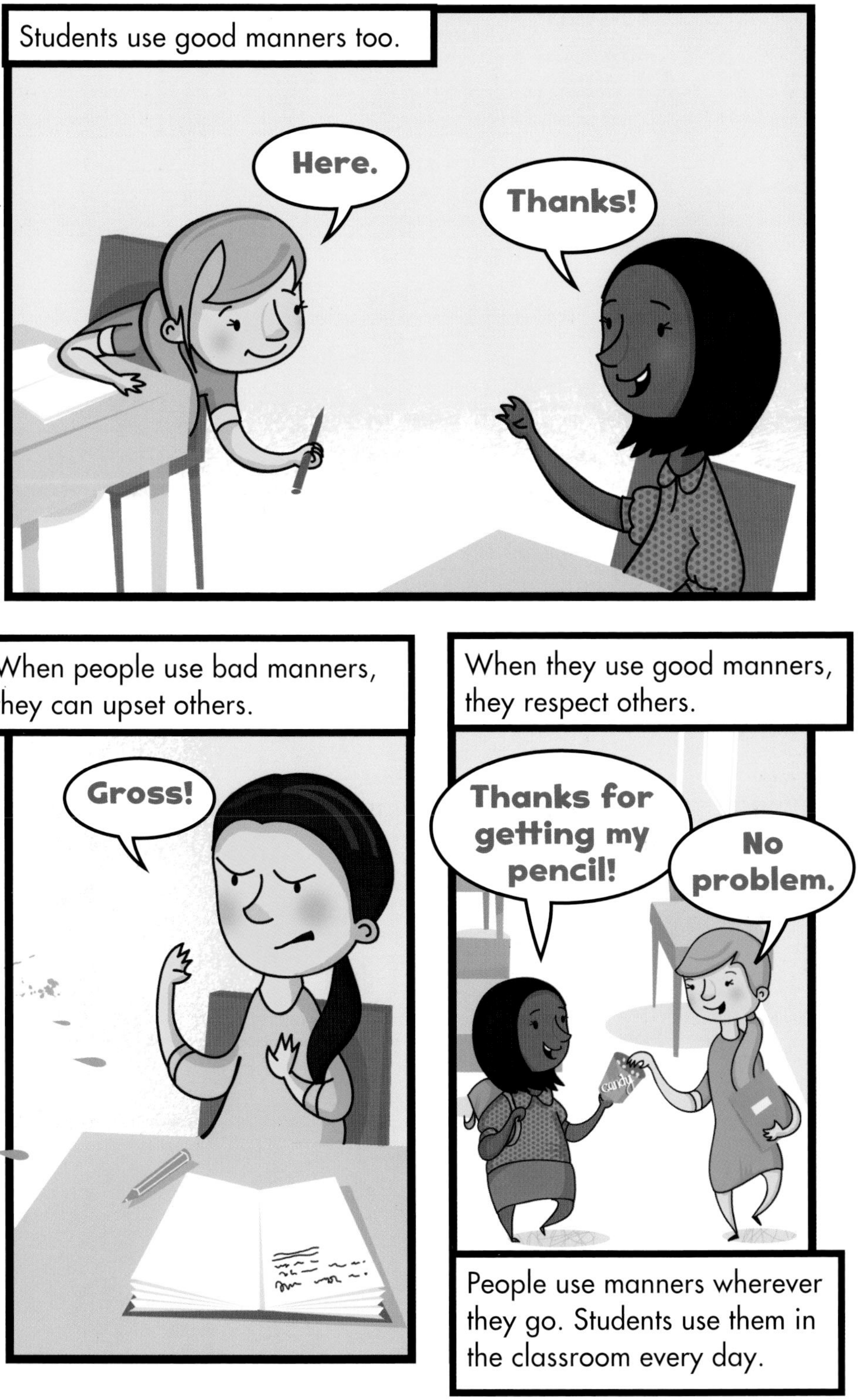
Students use good manners too.
Here.
Thanks!
When people use bad manners, they can upset others.
Gross!
When they use good manners, they respect others.
Thanks for getting my pencil!
No problem.
candy
People use manners wherever they go. Students use them in the classroom every day.

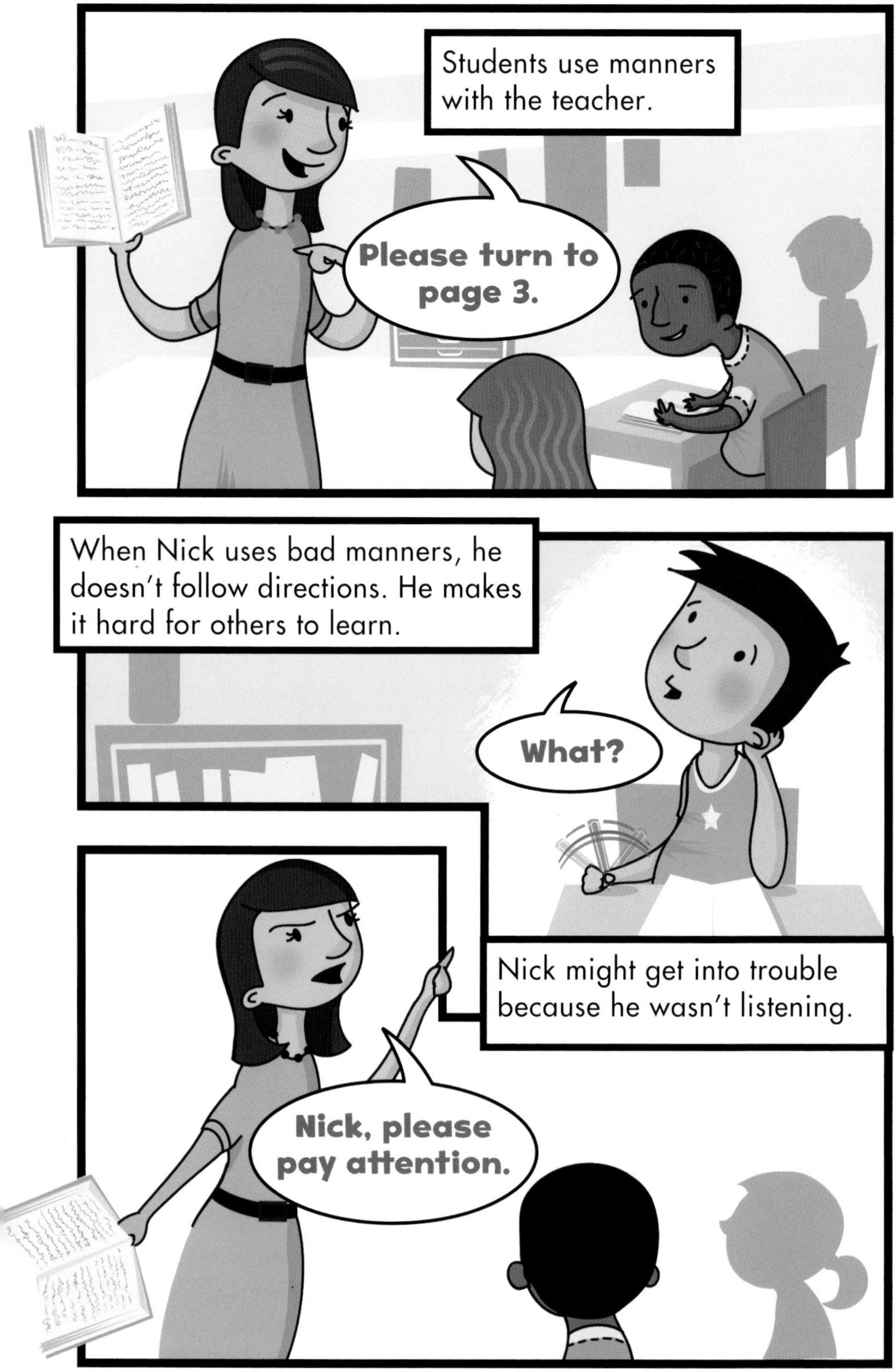

Students use manners with the teacher.
Please turn to page 3.
When Nick uses bad manners, he doesn't follow directions. He makes it hard for others to learn.
What?
Nick might get into trouble because he wasn't listening.
Nick, please pay attention.

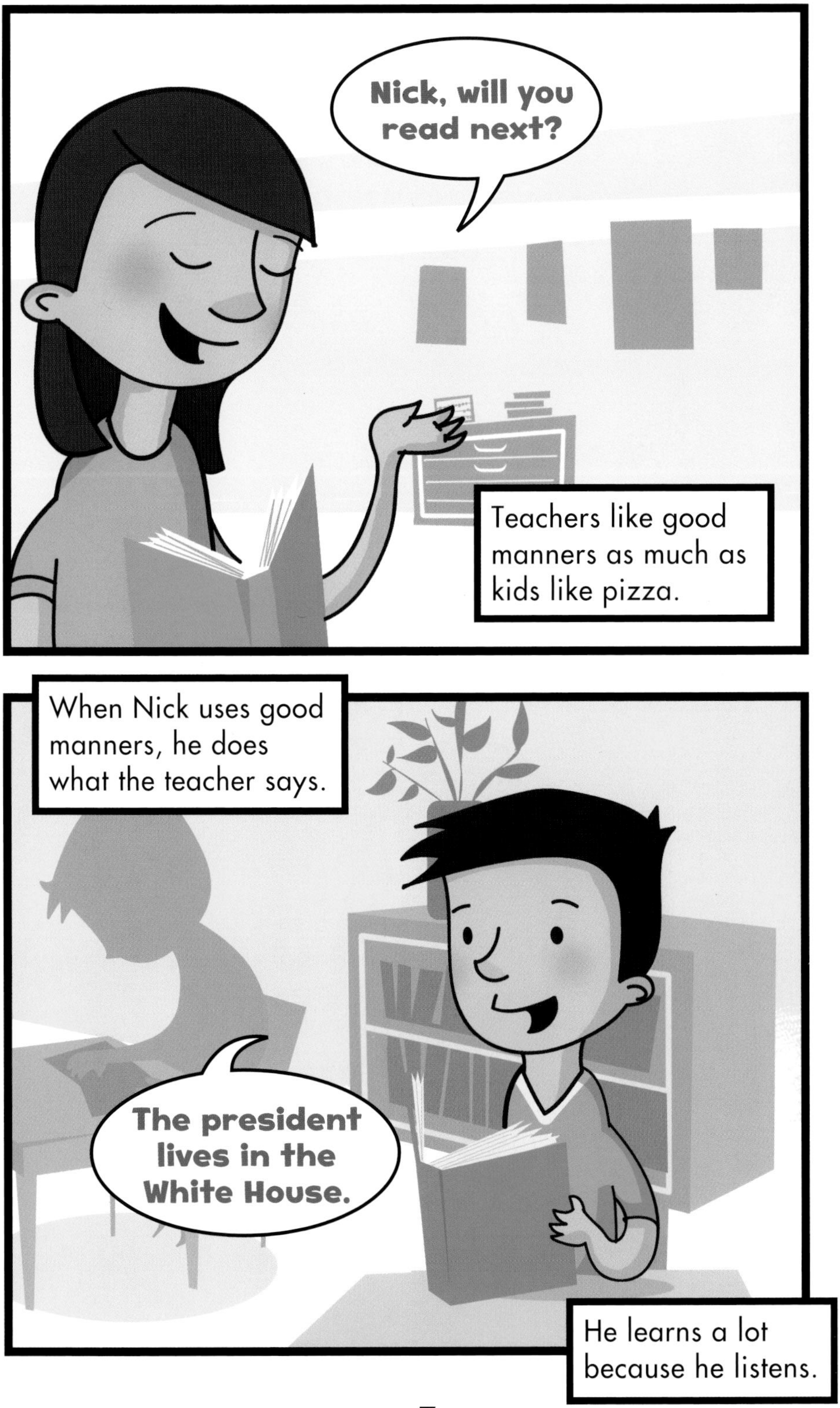
Nick, will you read next?
Teachers like good manners as much as kids like pizza.
When Nick uses good manners, he does what the teacher says.
The president lives in the White House.
He learns a lot because he listens.

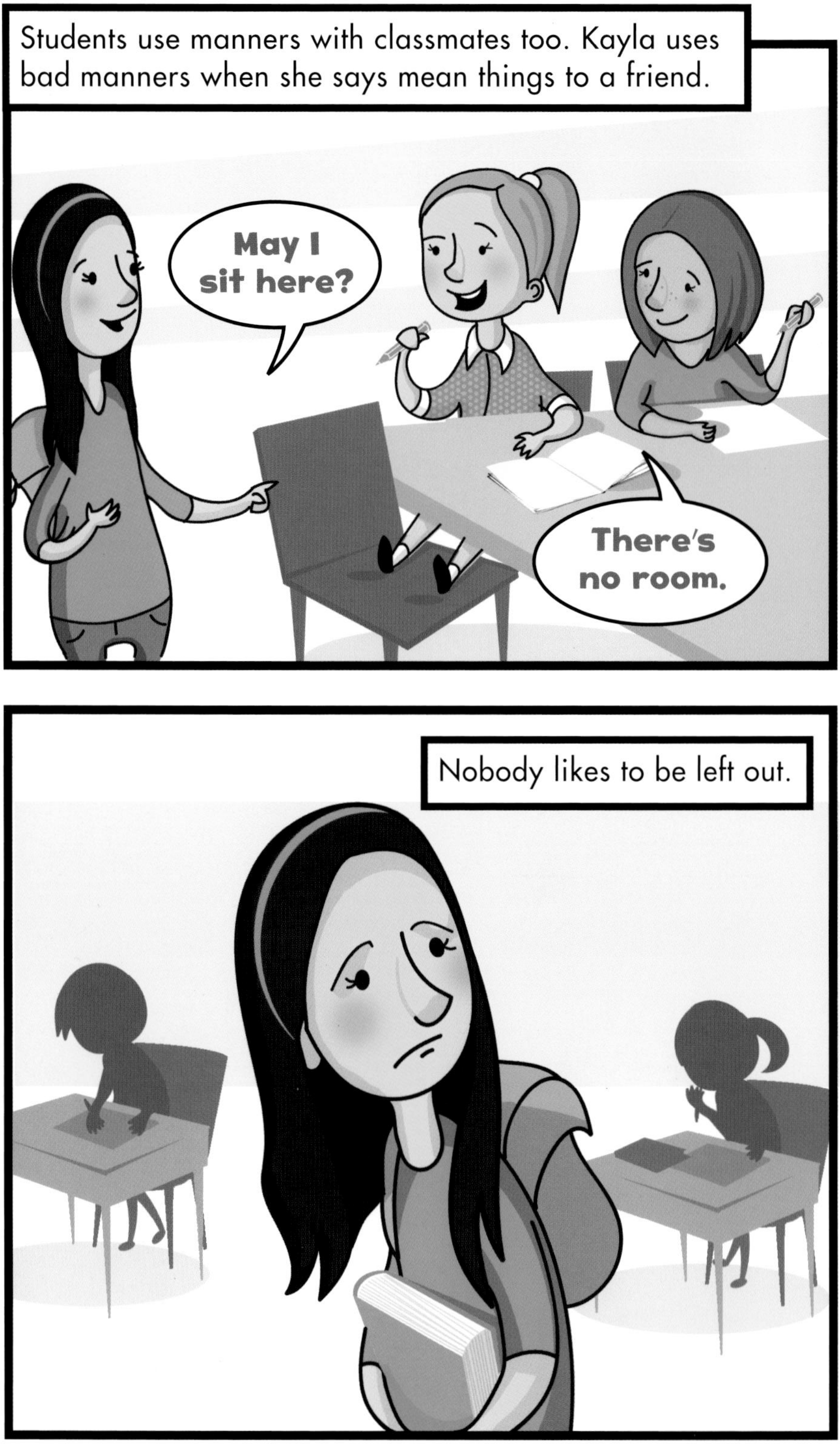
Students use manners with classmates too. Kayla uses bad manners when she says mean things to a friend.
May I sit here?
There's no room.
Nobody likes to be left out.

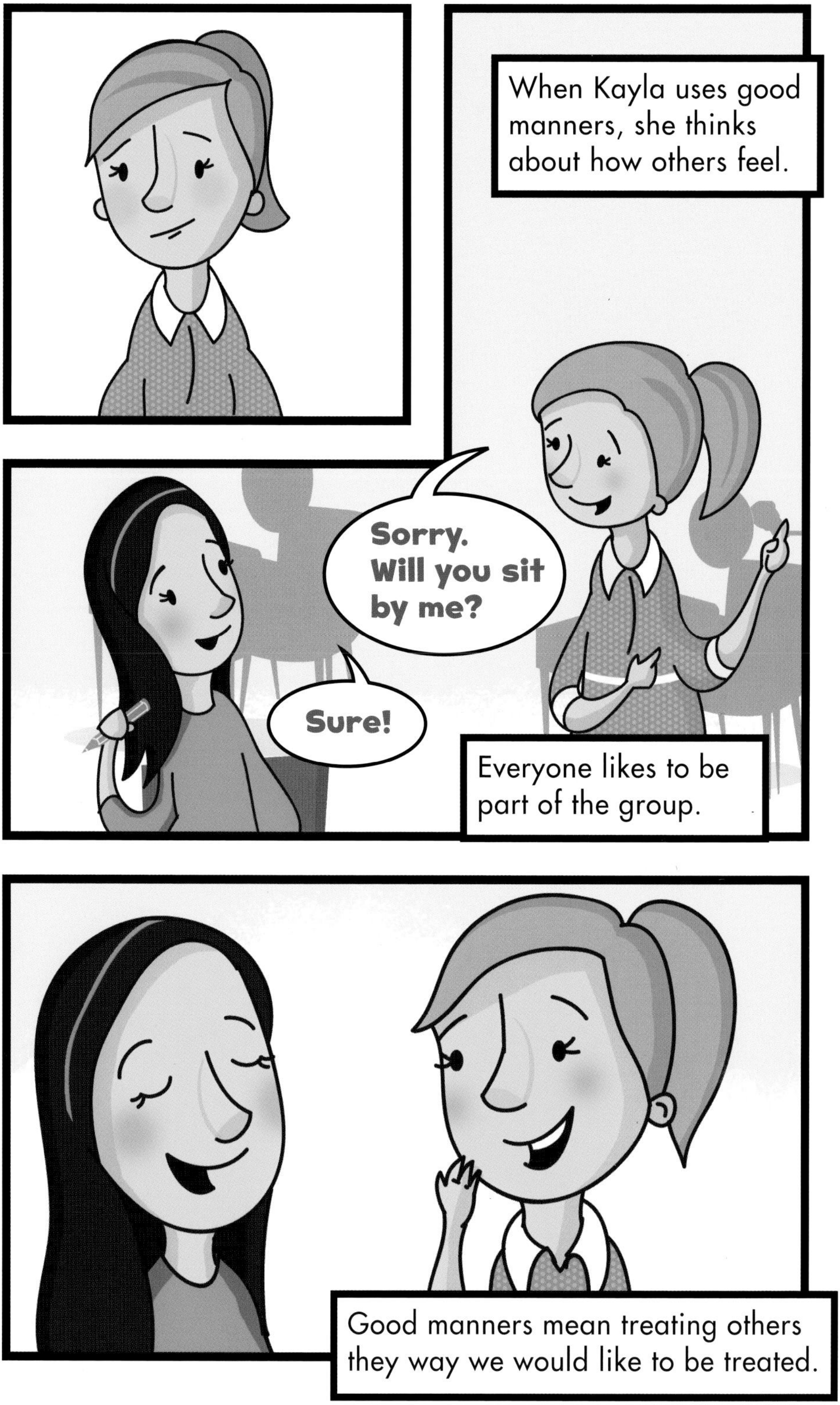
When Kayla uses good manners, she thinks about how others feel.
Sorry. Will you sit by me?
Sure!
Everyone likes to be part of the group.
Good manners mean treating others they way we would like to be treated.

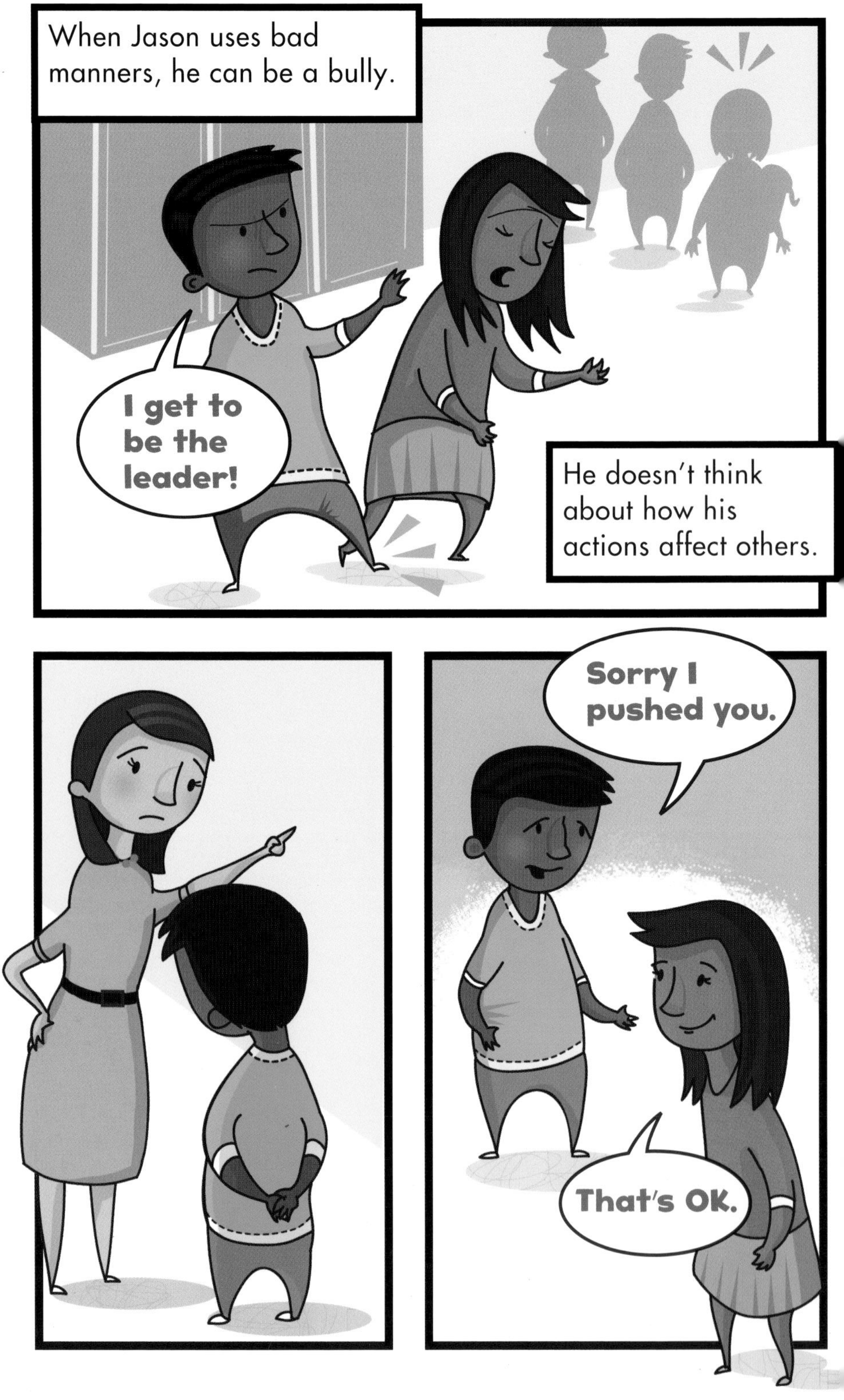
When Jason uses bad manners, he can be a bully.
I get to be the leader!
He doesn't think about how his actions affect others.
Sorry I pushed you.
That's OK.

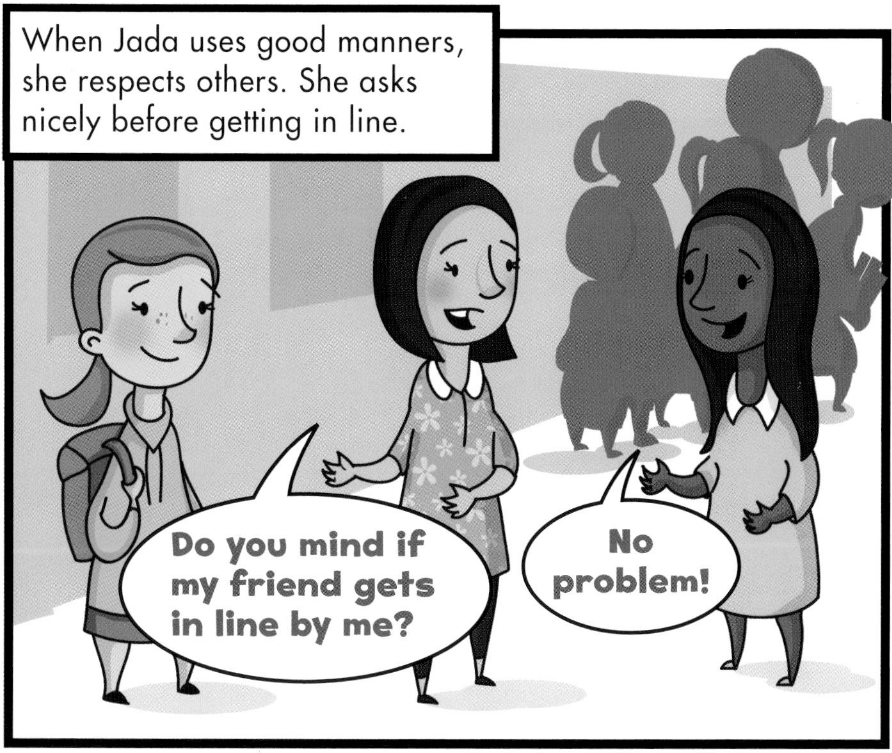
When Jada uses good manners, she respects others. She asks nicely before getting in line.
Do you mind if my friend gets in line by me?
No problem!

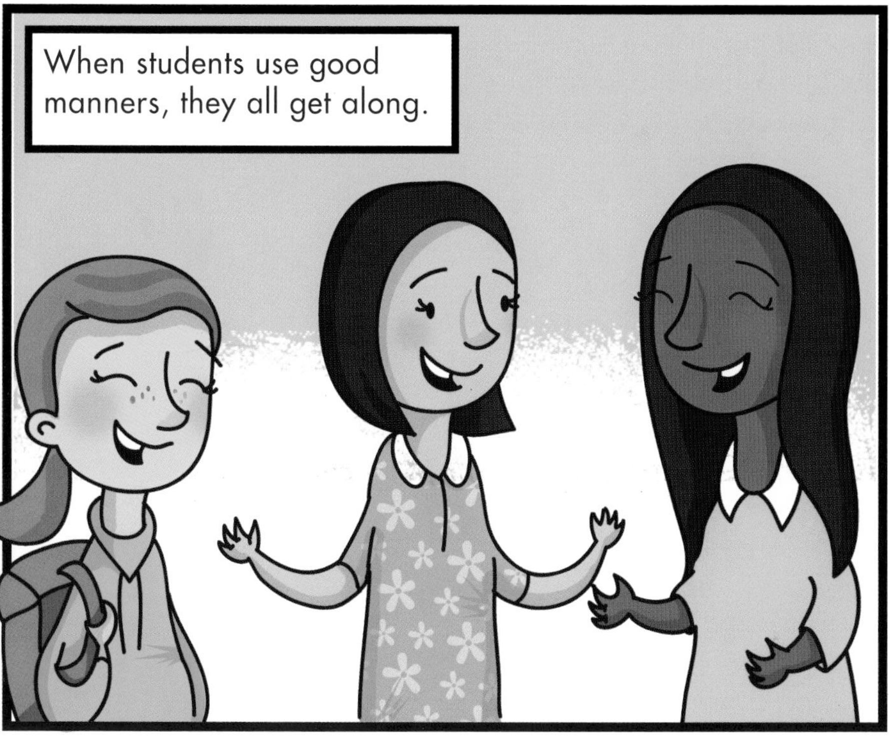
When students use good manners, they all get along.

# MANNERS AND STUFF

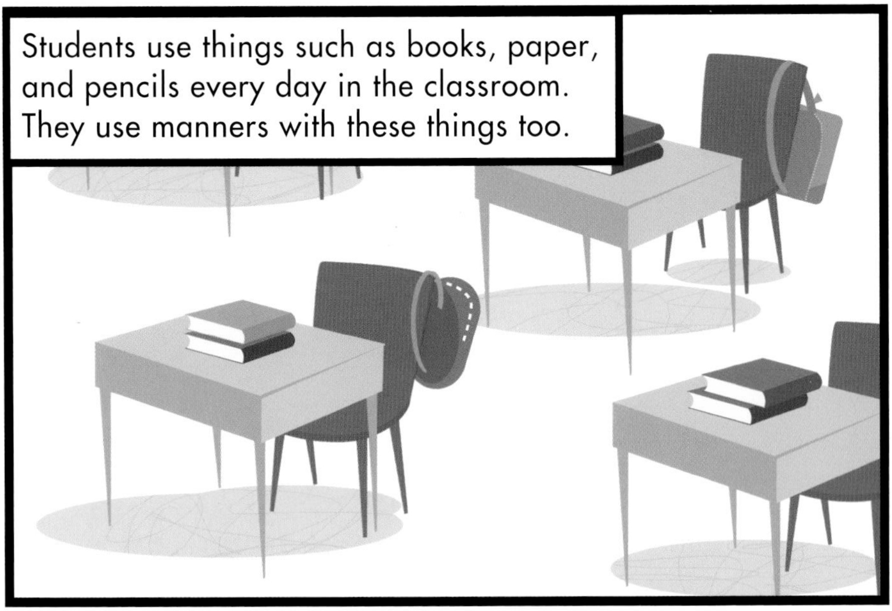
Students use things such as books, paper, and pencils every day in the classroom. They use manners with these things too.

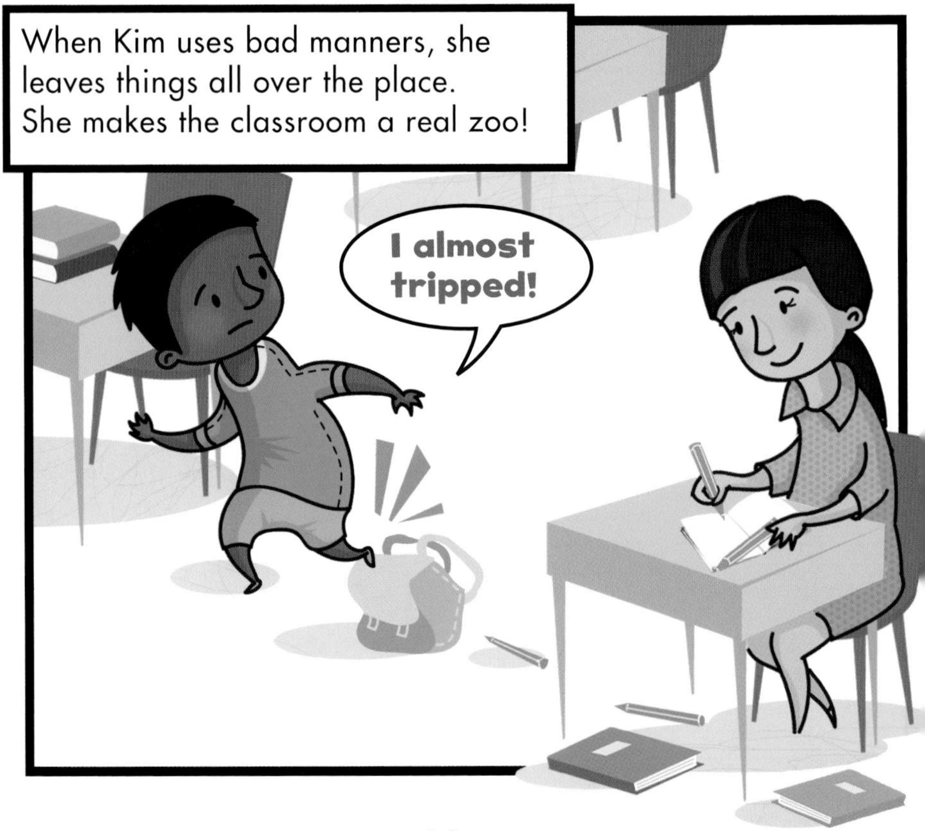
When Kim uses bad manners, she leaves things all over the place. She makes the classroom a real zoo!
I almost tripped!

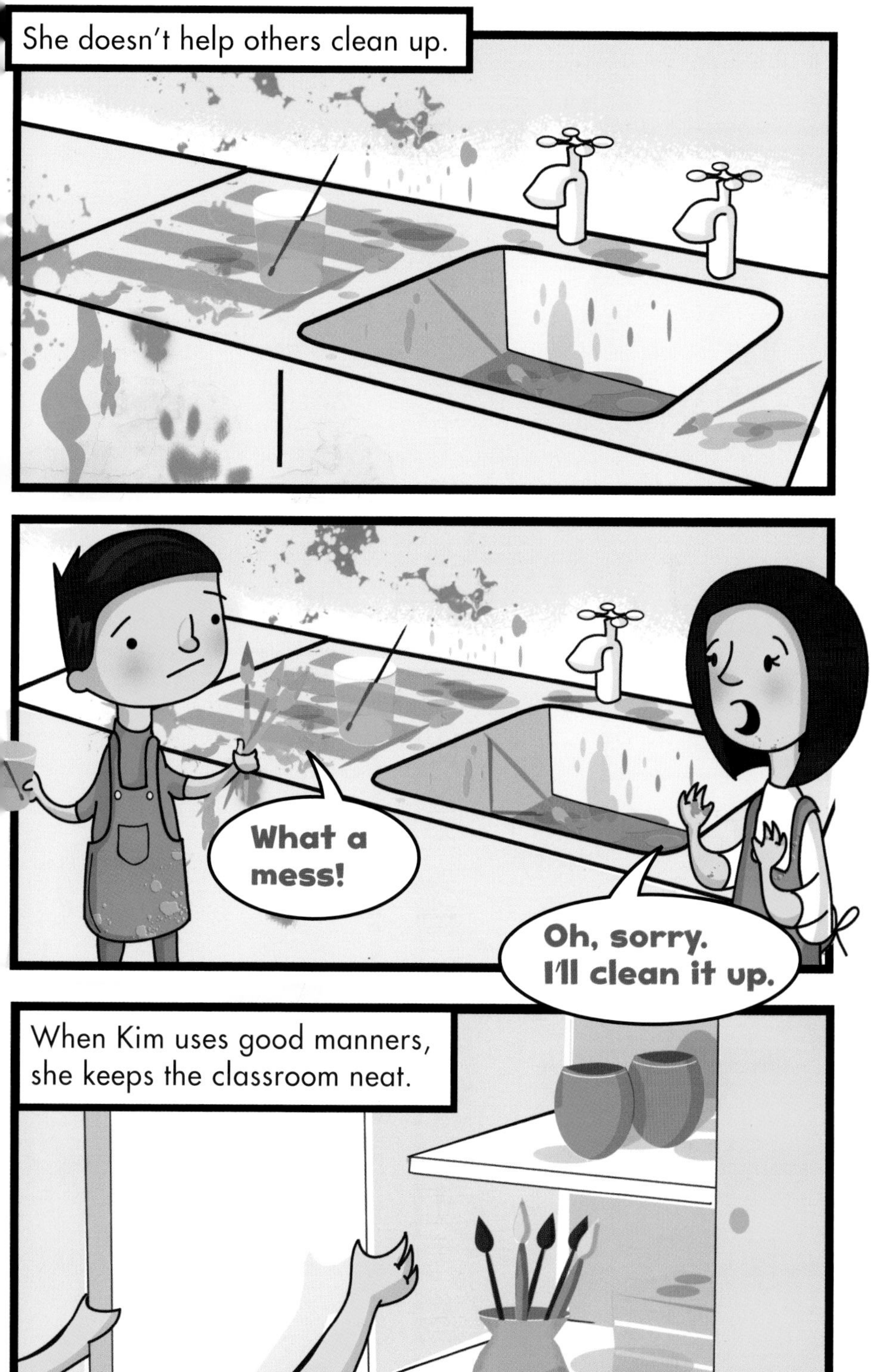
She doesn't help others clean up.
What a mess!
Oh, sorry. I'll clean it up.
When Kim uses good manners, she keeps the classroom neat.

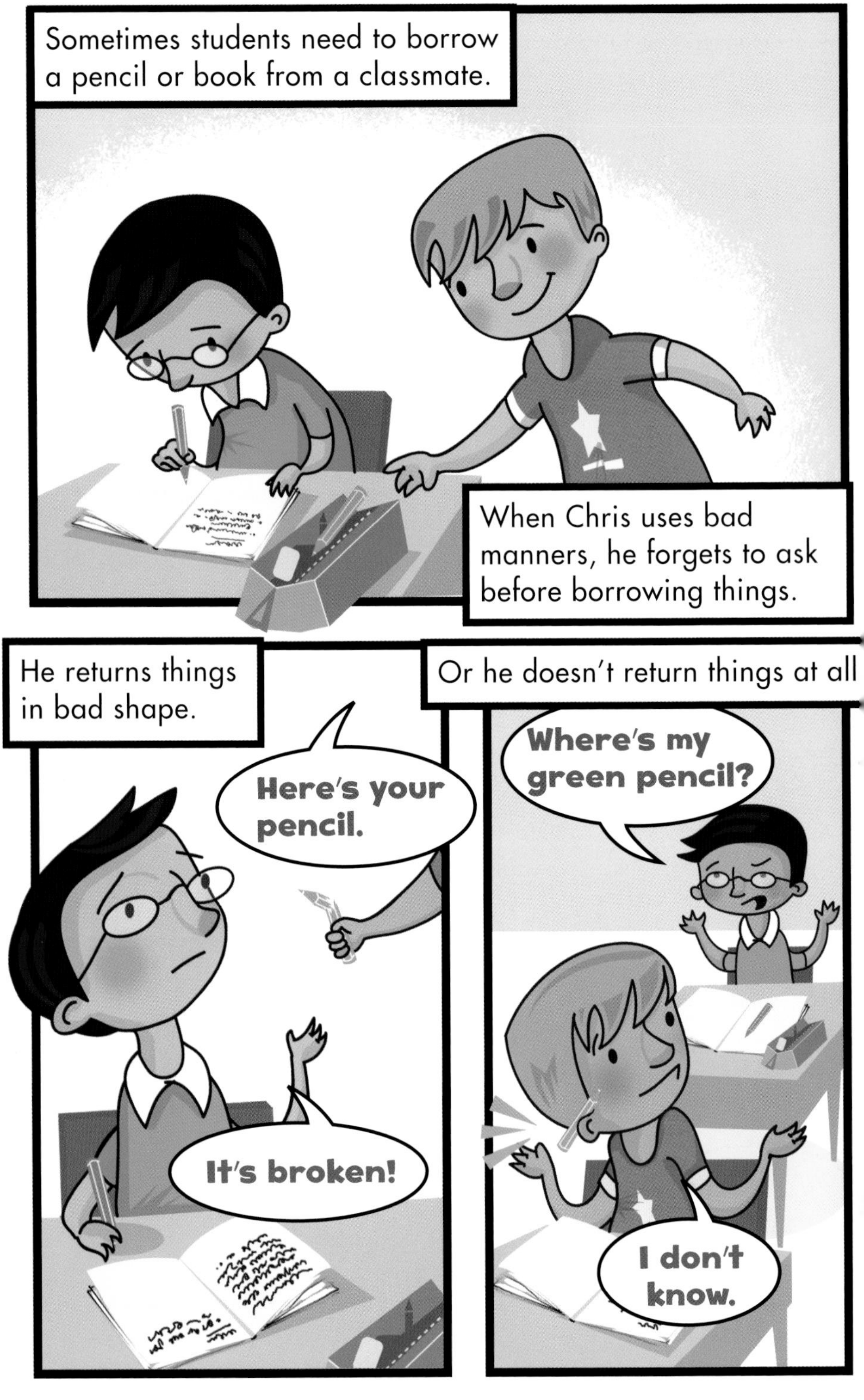

Sometimes students need to borrow a pencil or book from a classmate.
When Chris uses bad manners, he forgets to ask before borrowing things.
He returns things in bad shape.
Here's your pencil.
It's broken!
Or he doesn't return things at all
Where's my green pencil?
I don't know.

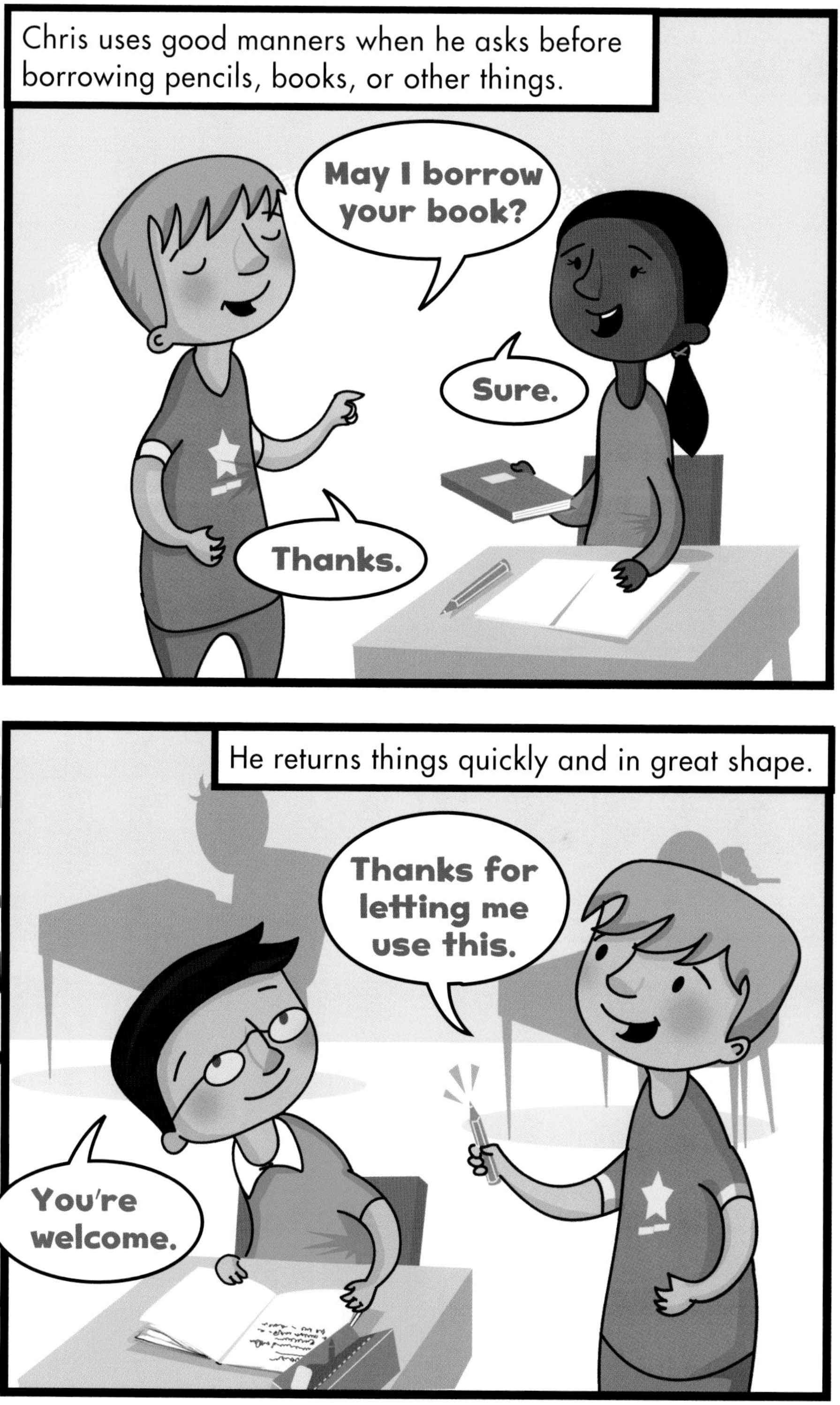
Chris uses good manners when he asks before borrowing pencils, books, or other things.
May I borrow your book?
Sure.
Thanks.
He returns things quickly and in great shape.
Thanks for letting me use this.
You're welcome.

# QUIET, PLEASE

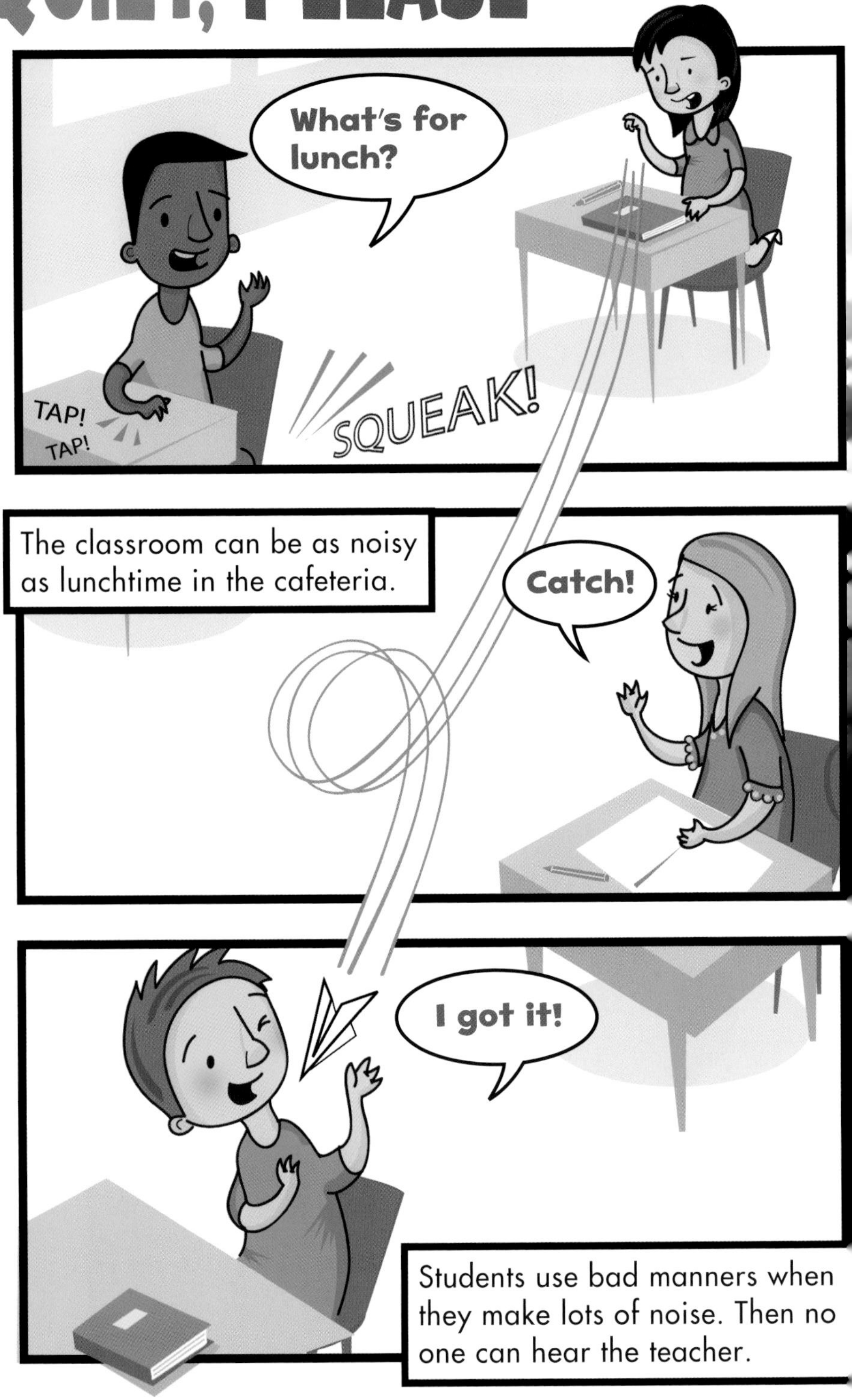
What's for lunch?
TAP! TAP!
SQUEAK!
The classroom can be as noisy as lunchtime in the cafeteria.
Catch!
I got it!
Students use bad manners when they make lots of noise. Then no one can hear the teacher.

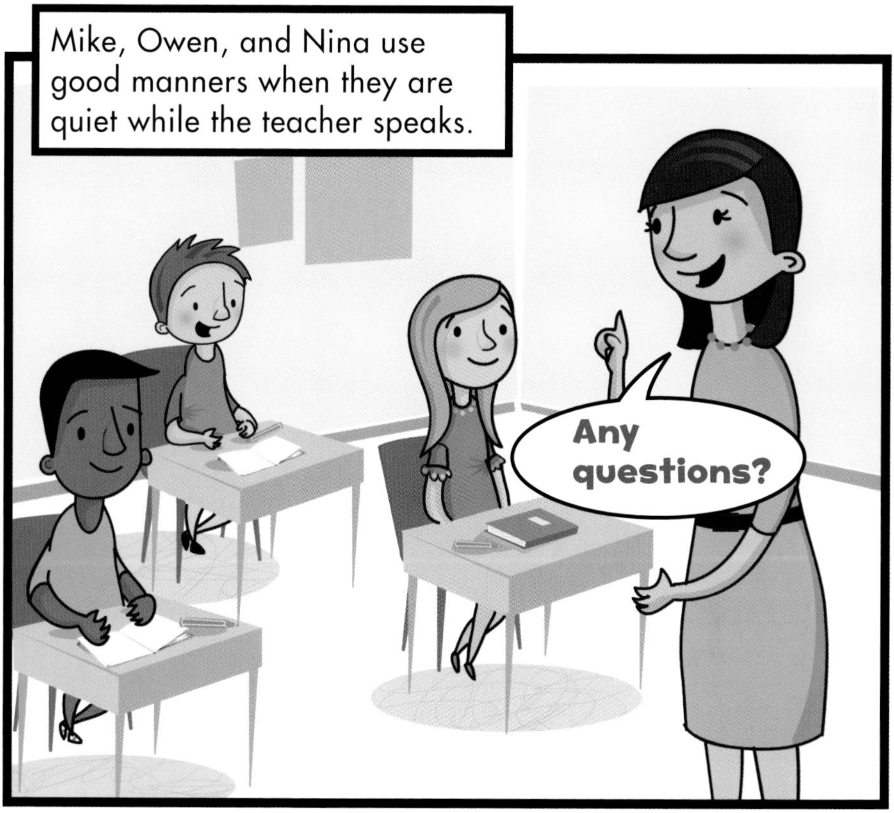
Mike, Owen, and Nina use good manners when they are quiet while the teacher speaks.
Any questions?

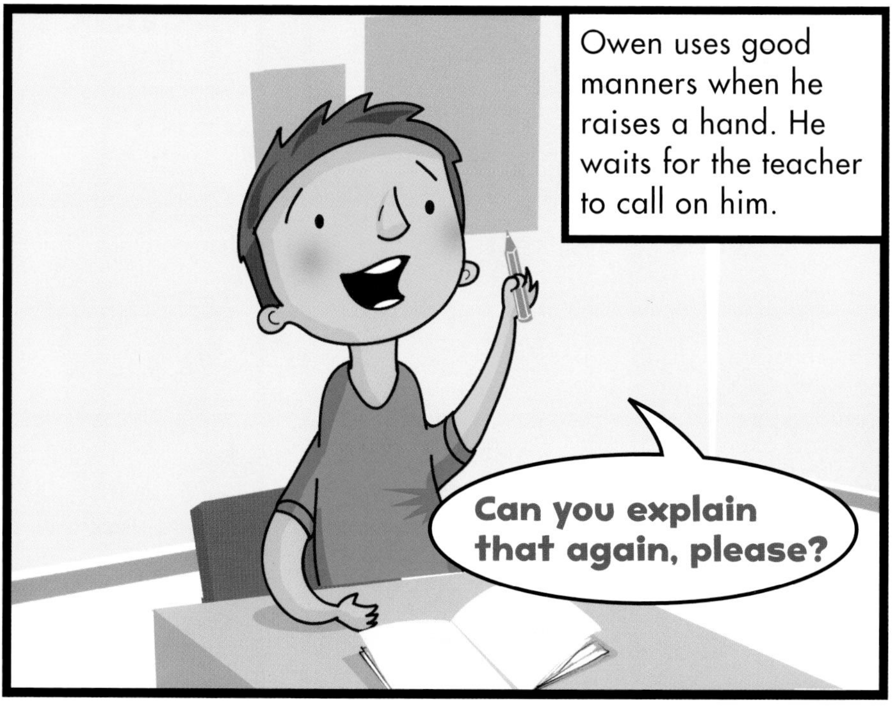
Owen uses good manners when he raises a hand. He waits for the teacher to call on him.
Can you explain that again, please?

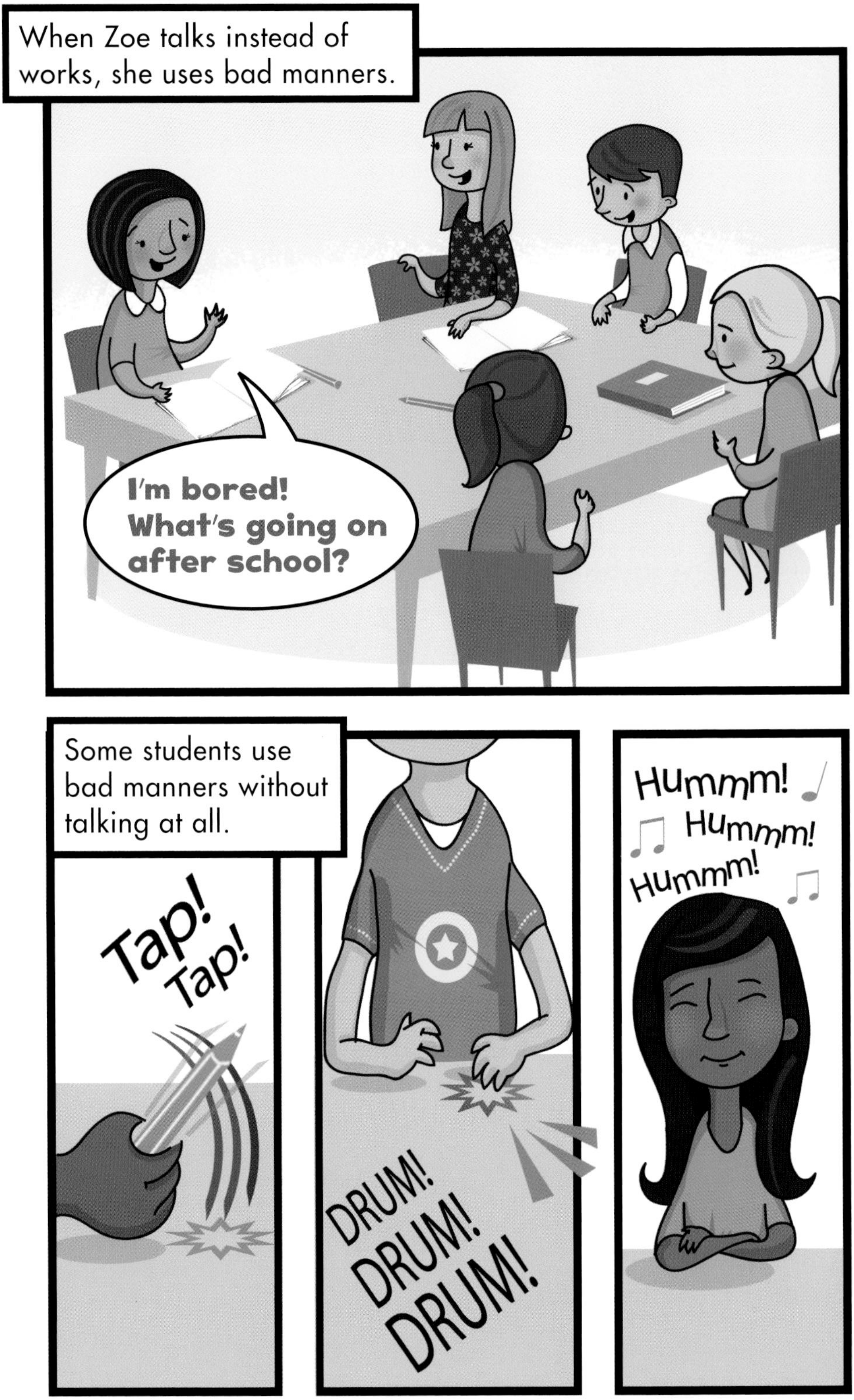
When Zoe talks instead of works, she uses bad manners.
I'm bored! What's going on after school?
Some students use bad manners without talking at all.
Tap! Tap!
DRUM! DRUM! DRUM!
Hummm! Hummm! Hummm!

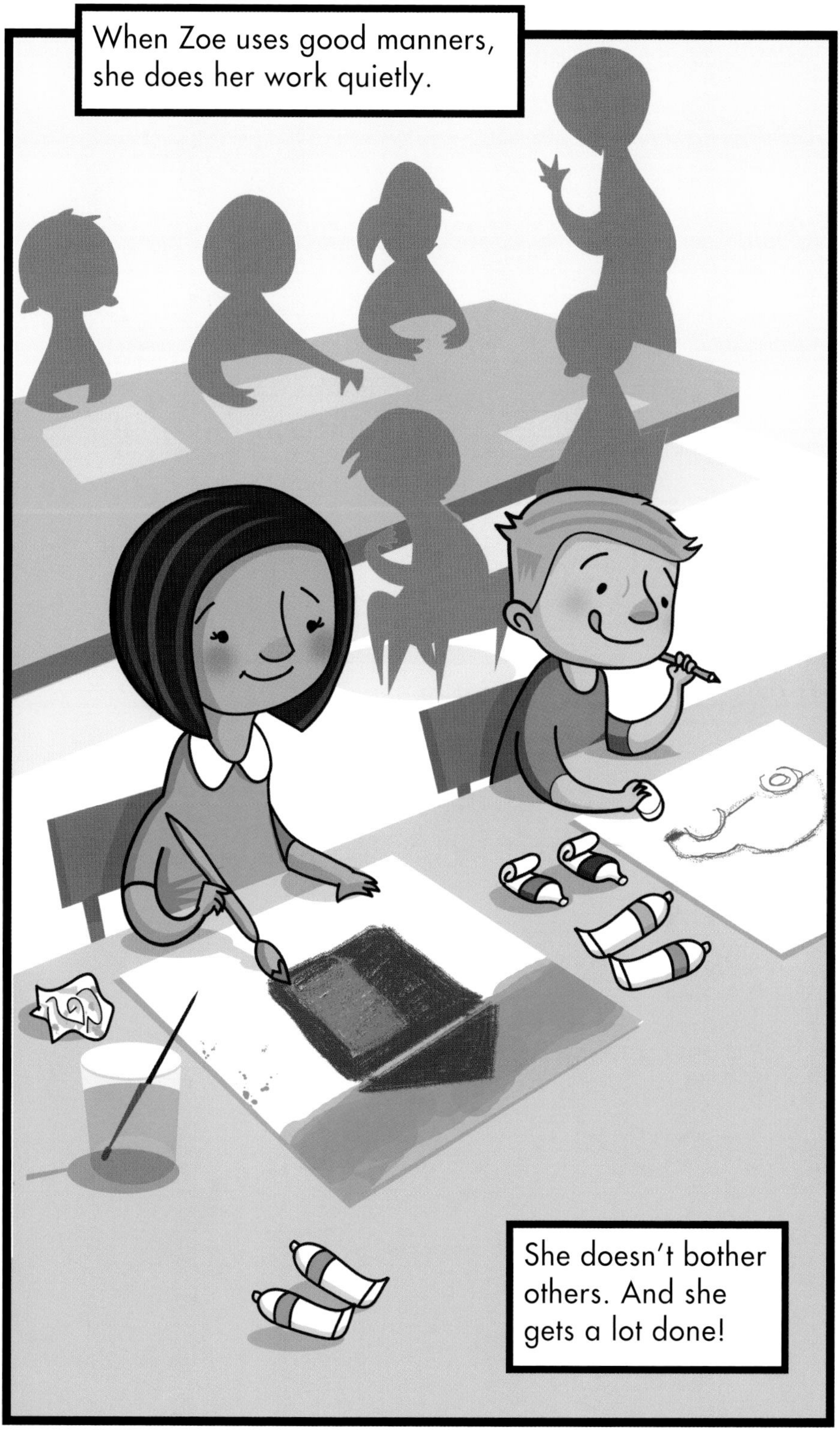
When Zoe uses good manners, she does her work quietly.
She doesn't bother others. And she gets a lot done!

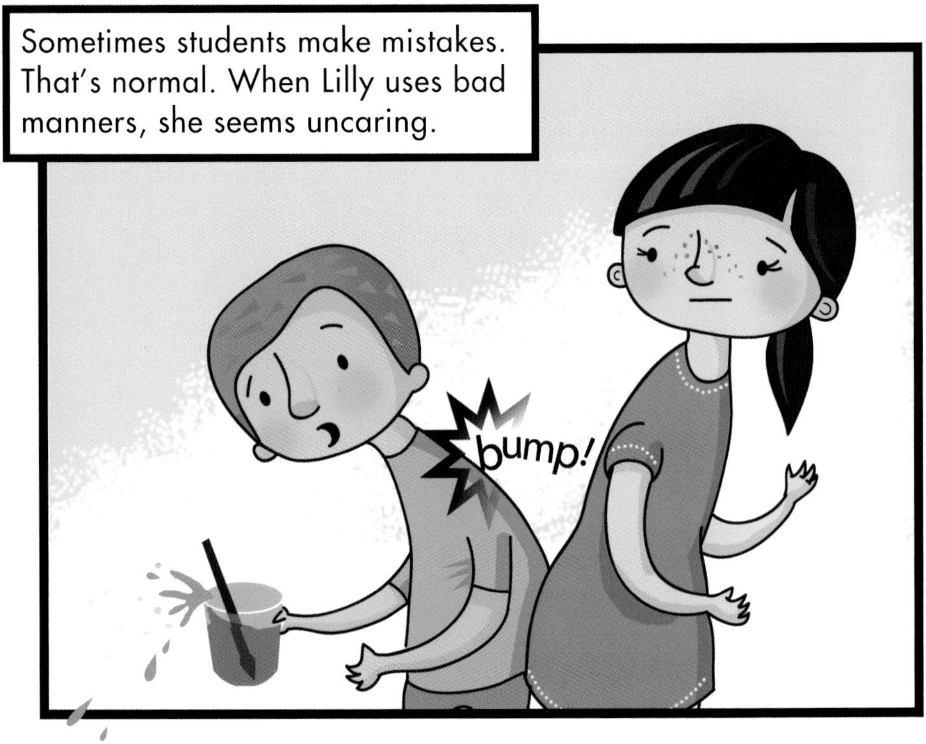
Sometimes students make mistakes. That's normal. When Lilly uses bad manners, she seems uncaring.
bump!

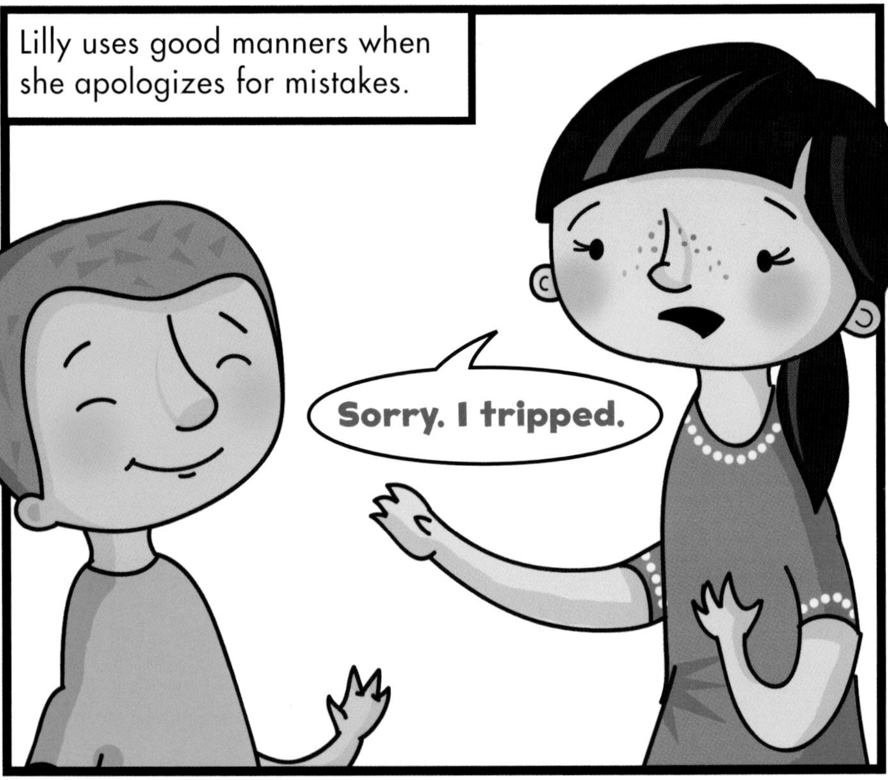
Lilly uses good manners when she apologizes for mistakes.
Sorry. I tripped.

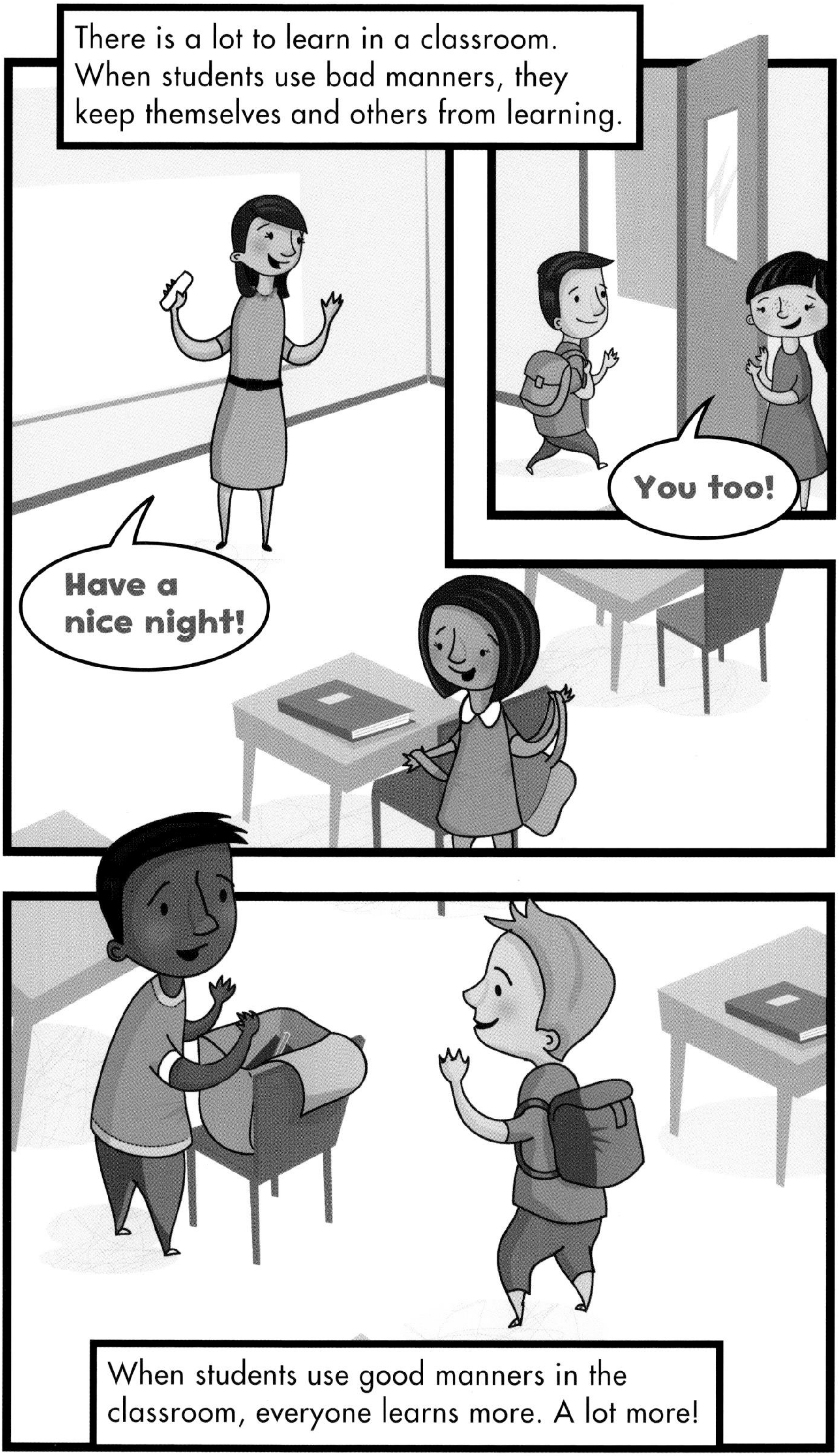
There is a lot to learn in a classroom. When students use bad manners, they keep themselves and others from learning.
You too!
Have a nice night!
When students use good manners in the classroom, everyone learns more. A lot more!

# GLOSSARY

**borrow**—to use something for a certain amount of time before returning it

**bully**—someone who uses strength to harm those who are weaker

**cafeteria**—a place in a school where students eat

**classmate**—someone who is in the same class

**respect**—to show you care; respect means to treat others the way you would like to be treated

# READ MORE

**Goldberg, Whoopi.** *Whoopi's Big Book of Manners.* New York: Hyperion Books for Children, 2006.

**Keller, Laurie,** *Do Unto Otters: A Book About Manners.* New York: Henry Holt, 2007.

**Tourville, Amanda Doering.** *Manners in the Lunchroom.* Way to Be! Minneapolis: Picture Window Books, 2009.

# INTERNET SITES

FactHound offers a safe, fun way to find Internet sites related to this book. All of the sites on FactHound have been researched by our staff.

Here's all you do:

Visit *www.facthound.com*

Type in this code: 9781429653336

Check out projects, games and lots more at
**www.capstonekids.com**

# INDEX



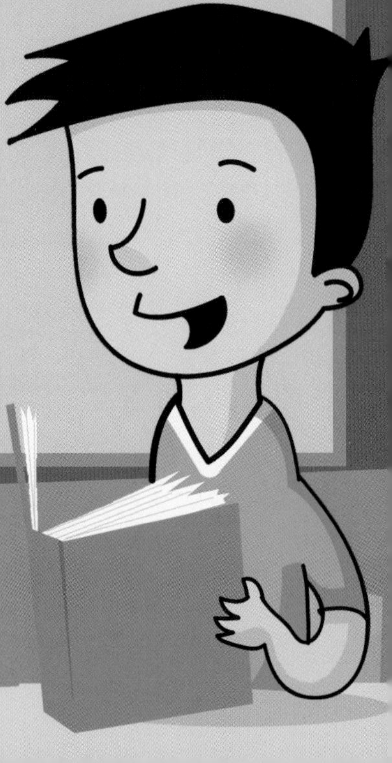

FIRST GRAPHICS

# Manners Matter

## TITLES IN THIS SET:

MANNERS MATTER IN THE CLASSROOM

MANNERS MATTER IN THE LIBRARY

MANNERS MATTER ON A FIELD TRIP

MANNERS MATTER ON THE PLAYGROUND